# Relaxing Anti-Stress Flowers: Coloring Book for Adults

**Hello Friend.**

**Welcome to the book "Relaxing Anti-stress Flowers: Coloring Book for Adults", a great opportunity for you to immerse yourself happily in the colors and shapes of the most beautiful and varied flowers that exist.**

**Immerse yourself in the therapeutic embrace of flowers and their dazzling, exquisitely drawn colors, where each petal becomes a brushstroke, or a fill of calm and joy on the canvas of your mind.**

**This coloring book is not just a collection of images; is a journey through the calming landscapes of nature, inviting you to relax, de-stress and rediscover the joy of coloring. Let the vibrant hues bring these flowers to life as you embark on a meditative adventure that rejuvenates the spirit and brings tranquility to your soul.**

**Embrace the therapeutic power of art and nature as you turn the pages of "Relaxing Anti-Stress Flowers", your passport to serenity and well-being.**

**This book was made especially for you. Come and immerse yourself in the colors and flowers.**

**Be Happy!**

**TUTOES Publications**
**2024**

# Relaxing Anti-Stress Flowers: Coloring Book for Adults

# This Book Belongs to:

TUTOES©
Publications

# Test Color Page

# Sunflower

# Sunflowers

# Roses

# Roses

# Tulips Flowers

# Tulips Flowers

# Carnation Flowers

# Carnation Flowers

# Cherry Blossom Flowers

# Cherry Blossom Flowers

# Cherry Blossom Flowers

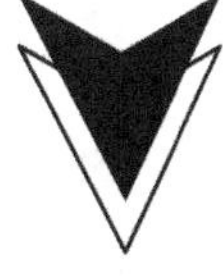

# Hibiscus Flower

# Hibiscus Flowers

# Hydrangeas Flowers

# Hydrangeas Flowers

# Gerbera Flowers

# Gerbera Flowers

# Gerbera Flowers

# Lily Flowers

# Lily Flowers

# Lotus Flowers

# Lotus Flowers

# Orchid Flowers

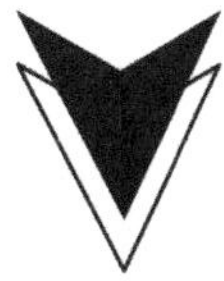

# Orchid Flowers

# Orchid Flowers

# Daysi Flowers

# Daisy Flowers

# Cherry Blossom Flowers

# Lotus Flowers

# Roses

# Sunflowers

# Test Color Page

# Relaxing Anti-Stress Flowers: Coloring Book for Adults

**TUTOES**[©]


**TUTOES Publications**
**2024**